**The Urbana Free Library**

To renew: call **217-367-4057**
or go to **urbanafreelibrary.org**
and select **My Account**

# COOL Chicken Recipes

## Main Dishes for Beginning Chefs

Alex Kuskowski

**Checkerboard
Library**

An Imprint of Abdo Publishing
abdopublishing.com

# abdopublishing.com

Published by Abdo Publishing, a division of ABDO, PO Box 398166, Minneapolis, Minnesota 55439. Copyright © 2017 by Abdo Consulting Group, Inc. International copyrights reserved in all countries. No part of this book may be reproduced in any form without written permission from the publisher. Checkerboard Library™ is a trademark and logo of Abdo Publishing.

Printed in the United States of America,
North Mankato, Minnesota
102016
012017

Design and Production: Mighty Media, Inc.
Series Editor: Liz Salzmann
Photo Credits: Mighty Media, Inc.; Shutterstock

The following manufacturers/names appearing in this book are trademarks: Argo®, Essential Everyday™, Frank's®, Kemps®, Marukan®, Old London®, Oster®, Pyrex®, Roundy's®, Swanson®

**Publisher's Cataloging-in-Publication Data**

Names: Kuskowski, Alex, author.
Title: Cool chicken recipes: main dishes for beginning chefs / by Alex Kuskowski.
Other titles: Main dishes for beginning chefs
Description: Minneapolis, MN : Abdo Publishing, 2017. | Series: Cool main dish recipes | Includes bibliographical references and index.
Identifiers: LCCN 2016944834 | ISBN 9781680781335 (lib. bdg.) | ISBN 9781680775532 (ebook)
Subjects: LCSH: Cooking--Juvenile literature. | Dinners and dining--Juvenile literature. | Entrees (Cooking)--Juvenile literature. | One-dish meals--Juvenile literature.
Classification: DDC 641.82--dc23
LC record available at http://lccn.loc.gov/2016944834

## TO ADULT HELPERS

Get cooking! This is your chance to help a budding chef. Being able to cook meals is a life skill. Learning to cook gives kids new experiences and helps them gain confidence. These recipes are designed to help kids learn how to cook on their own. They may need more assistance on some recipes than others. Be there to offer guidance when they need it. Encourage them to do as much as they can on their own. Make sure to have rules for cleanup. There should always be adult supervision when kids are using sharp utensils or a hot oven or stove.

## SAFETY FIRST!

Some recipes call for activities or ingredients that require caution. If you see these symbols, ask an adult for help.

### HOT STUFF!
This recipe requires the use of a stove or oven. Always use pot holders when handling hot objects.

### SUPER SHARP!
This recipe includes the use of a sharp utensil, such as a knife or grater.

### NUT ALERT!
Some people can get very sick if they eat nuts. If you cook something with nuts, let people know!

# Contents

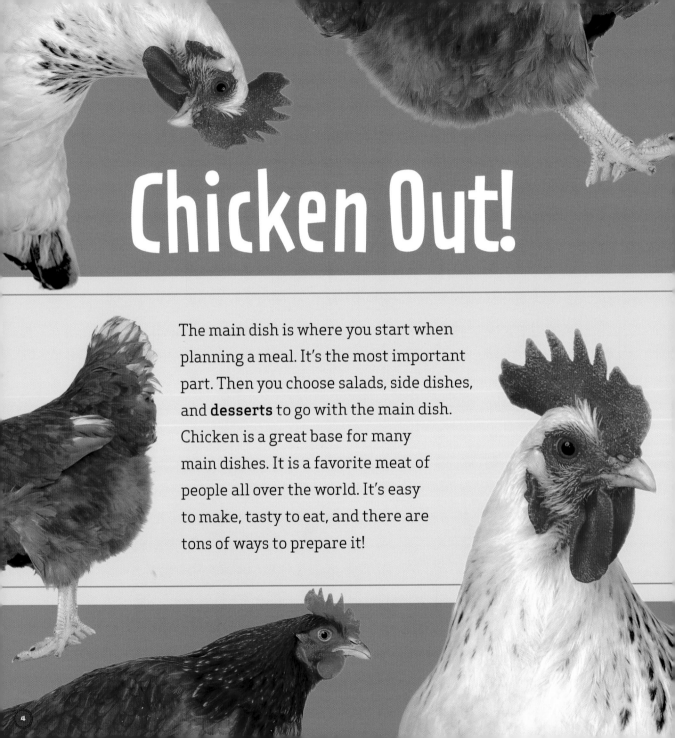

# Chicken Out!

The main dish is where you start when planning a meal. It's the most important part. Then you choose salads, side dishes, and **desserts** to go with the main dish. Chicken is a great base for many main dishes. It is a favorite meat of people all over the world. It's easy to make, tasty to eat, and there are tons of ways to prepare it!

There are chicken recipes to **entice** every taste bud. Make spicy chicken quesadillas. Fry up some crunchy chicken strips. Bake a **savory** spinach quiche.

Try all of the chicken recipes in this book. Then think of your own ways to cook chicken. The possibilities are endless!

# I ♥ CHICKEN

## what's not to love about chicken?

It's easy to cook and it always tastes yummy! Here are a few tips and tricks to make your chicken dishes even better.

## PICKING THE MEAT

Boneless, skinless chicken breasts are the easiest meat to cook. They are easy to cut and prepare. Always keep chicken in the refrigerator or freezer.

## HANDLING THE MEAT

**Thaw** frozen chicken in a bowl filled with water. Wash thawed chicken under running water. Pat it dry with a towel.

## KEEP IT CLEAN

Wash your hands before and after touching the meat. Wash any **utensils** that touched raw chicken separately from other dishes.

## CUTTING THE MEAT

Put uncooked boneless, skinless chicken on a cutting board. Use a sharp knife to cut it. Always cut away from your fingers.

## COOKING THE MEAT

Cook the chicken until there is no pink left. Pink meat or pink juice means the chicken is not cooked enough.

# COOKING BASICS

## Ask Permission

- Before you cook, ask **permission** to use the kitchen, cooking tools, and ingredients.

- If you'd like to do something yourself, say so! Just remember to be safe.

- If you would like help, ask for it!

## Be Prepared

- Be organized. Knowing where everything is makes cooking safer and more fun!

- Read the directions all the way through before starting a recipe. Follow the directions in order.

- The most important ingredient is preparation! Make sure you have everything you'll need.

## Be Smart, Be Safe

- Never cook if you are home alone.

- Always have an adult nearby for hot jobs, such as using the oven or the stove.

- Have an adult around when using a sharp tool, such as a knife or a grater. Always be careful when using these tools!

- Remember to turn pot handles toward the back of the stove. That way you won't accidentally knock the pots over.

## Be Neat, Be Clean

- Start with clean hands, clean tools, and a clean work surface.

- Tie back long hair to keep it out of the food.

- Wear comfortable clothing and roll up your sleeves.

- Put extra ingredients and tools away when you're done.

- Wash all the dishes and **utensils**. Clean up your workspace.

# COOKING TERMS

### CUBE

Cube means to cut something into bite-size squares.

### GREASE
Grease means to coat something with butter or cooking spray.

### MINCE

Mince means to cut or chop something into very tiny pieces.

### SOAK
Soak means to let something sit in a liquid.

### SPRINKLE
Sprinkle means to drop small pieces of something.

## DICE
Dice means to cut something into small squares.

## DRIZZLE
Drizzle means to slowly pour a liquid over something.

## SHRED
Shred means to cut small pieces of something using a grater.

## SLICE
Slice means to cut something into pieces of the same thickness.

## STIR
Stir means to mix ingredients together, usually with a large spoon.

## WHISK
Whisk means to beat quickly by hand with a whisk or a fork.

# INGREDIENTS

Here are some of the ingredients you will need.

avocado

bell pepper

cheeses

cherry tomatoes

chicken breasts & wings

chicken broth

garlic

half-and-half

hot sauce

mixed salad greens

shredded coconut

soy sauce

spinach

sweet chili pepper

bread crumbs

butter

buttermilk

cayenne pepper

cornflakes

cornstarch

cumin

flour tortillas

onion

paprika

pie shell

rice vinegar

etened condensed milk

teriyaki sauce

vegetable oil

walnuts

13

# TOOLS

Here are some of the tools you will need.

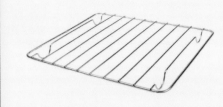
baking rack

baking sheet

large plastic zipper bags

large pot

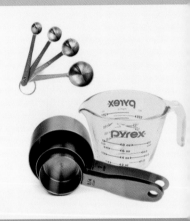
measuring cups & spoons

plate

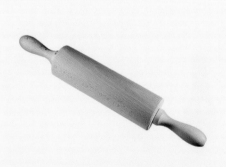
rolling pin

sharp knife

basting brush

cutting board

grill

mixing bowls

mixing spoon

pie pan

spatula

whisk

wooden skewers

# SPINACH
# Chicken Quiche

16

1 (9-inch) pie shell
1 cup shredded mozzarella
  cheese
1 cup diced cooked chicken
1 cup chopped spinach
1 cup chopped onion
¾ cup shredded cheddar
  cheese
3 eggs

¾ cup half-and-half
½ cup plain yogurt
¼ teaspoon salt
¼ teaspoon black pepper
½ teaspoon cumin

measuring cups
sharp knife
cutting board
measuring spoons
pie pan
mixing bowls
mixing spoon
whisk
pot holders

**1** Preheat the oven to 350 degrees. Put the pie shell in the pie pan. Sprinkle the mozzarella in the center of the pie shell.

**2** Put the chicken, spinach, onion, and cheddar in a large mixing bowl. Stir them together. Pour the mixture in the pie shell.

**3** Put the eggs, half-and-half, yogurt, salt, black pepper, and cumin in a small bowl. Whisk them together. Pour the egg mixture over the chicken mixture.

**4** Bake the quiche for 30 minutes. Turn it around. Bake for another 20 to 30 minutes. Take the quiche out of the oven. See if the middle is firm. If it's runny, bake it a little longer.

**5** Let the quiche cool for 15 minutes before serving.

1

2

3

# CRUNCHY
# Chicken Strips

## Bite into a dish with a snappy taste!

## INGREDIENTS

2 teaspoons salt
2 teaspoons black pepper
2 pounds chicken breast, sliced
⅓ cup orange juice
½ cup sweetened condensed milk
1 egg

1⅓ cups crushed cornflakes
1 cup shredded coconut
vegetable oil, for frying

## TOOLS

measuring spoons
measuring cups
sharp knife
cutting board
mixing bowls
whisk

electric frying pan
tongs
pot holders
paper towels
plate

1. Sprinkle salt and pepper on both sides of the chicken slices.

2. Put the orange juice, sweetened condensed milk, and egg in a bowl. Whisk them together. Put the cornflakes and coconut in another bowl. Stir them together.

3. Dip the chicken slices in the orange juice mixture. Then coat them with the cornflake mixture.

4. Put 2 inches (5 cm) of vegetable oil in the frying pan. Heat the oil on medium-high. Lay a paper towel on the plate. Fry the chicken for 3 to 4 minutes on one side. Turn the chicken over. Fry it for 3 to 4 more minutes. Place the chicken on the plate. Let it cool.

# SWEET & SOUR Chicken Bites

## Enjoy this bite-size chicken dish!

## INGREDIENTS

**SAUCE**
1 cup white sugar
4 tablespoons ketchup
½ cup rice vinegar
1 tablespoon soy sauce
1 teaspoon garlic salt

**CHICKEN**
3 chicken breasts, cubed
1 teaspoon salt
1 teaspoon black pepper
1 cup cornstarch
2 eggs
¼ cup vegetable oil

## TOOLS

measuring cups
measuring spoons
sharp knife
cutting board
mixing bowls
whisk

large plastic zipper bag
large pot
pot holders
tongs
square baking dish
mixing spoon

**1** Preheat the oven to 325 degrees. Put all of the sauce ingredients in a mixing bowl. Whisk them together.

**2** Sprinkle the salt and pepper over the chicken. Put the cornstarch and chicken in the plastic bag. Close the bag. Shake the bag to coat the chicken.

**3** Put the eggs in a bowl. Whisk them together. Dip the chicken in the eggs.

**4** Put the oil in the large pot. Heat it over medium-low heat. Add the chicken. Cook the chicken for 1 to 2 minutes on each side until brown.

**5** Put the chicken in the baking dish. Pour the sauce over the chicken. Stir to coat the chicken. Bake for 1 hour.

**2**

**4**

**5**

# SLICED
# Chicken Salad

Healthy deliciousness in every bite!

## INGREDIENTS

2 chicken breasts
3 tablespoons buttermilk
1 cup chopped walnuts
¾ cup bread crumbs
1 teaspoon salt
2 tablespoons vegetable oil
6 cups mixed salad greens
½ cup shredded Colby cheese
1 avocado, sliced

½ cup cherry tomatoes, chopped

**DRESSING**
⅓ cup lemon juice
½ cup olive oil
½ teaspoon garlic salt
¼ teaspoon salt
¼ teaspoon black pepper

## TOOLS

measuring spoons
measuring cups
sharp knife
cutting board
large plastic zipper bag
rolling pin

basting brush
mixing bowls
mixing spoons
large pot
pot holders
tongs
4 plates
jar

**1** Place the chicken in the plastic bag. Flatten the chicken with the rolling pin. Make it ¼ inch (0.25 cm) thick. Take the chicken out. Brush it with buttermilk.

**1**
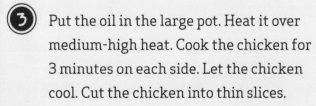
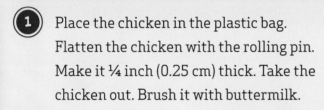

**2** Put the walnuts, bread crumbs, and salt in a mixing bowl. Stir them together. Dip the chicken in the mixture. Coat both sides of the chicken.

**3** Put the oil in the large pot. Heat it over medium-high heat. Cook the chicken for 3 minutes on each side. Let the chicken cool. Cut the chicken into thin slices.

**3**

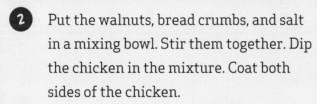

**4** Divide the salad greens between four plates. Divide the cheese, avocado, tomatoes, and chicken among the salads.

**4**

**5** Put the dressing ingredients in a jar. Shake it to mix the dressing. Drizzle dressing on top of the salads.

# BUFFALO
# Chicken Wings

A savory and delicious treat!

½ cup flour
¼ teaspoon paprika
¼ teaspoon cayenne
  pepper
¼ teaspoon salt
10 chicken wings
⅔ cup butter

⅓ cup hot sauce
non-stick cooking spray

measuring
  cups
measuring
  spoons
mixing bowls
mixing spoon
large plastic
  zipper bag

tongs
baking rack
baking sheet
pot holders
sharp knife

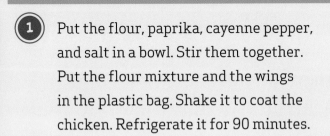

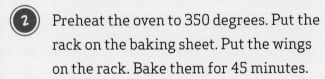

1. Put the flour, paprika, cayenne pepper, and salt in a bowl. Stir them together. Put the flour mixture and the wings in the plastic bag. Shake it to coat the chicken. Refrigerate it for 90 minutes.

2. Preheat the oven to 350 degrees. Put the rack on the baking sheet. Put the wings on the rack. Bake them for 45 minutes.

3. Turn the oven to 375 degrees. Take the wings out of the oven. Coat them with cooking spray. Bake for 20 more minutes.

4. Take the wings out of the oven. Cut into a wing. If it's pink inside, bake the wings a little longer. When done, remove the wings from the oven.

5. Put the butter in a bowl. Microwave it on low for 1 minute. Stir in the hot sauce. Coat the wings with the sauce.

1

2

5

# CHEESY
# Chicken Quesadilla

### You'll love every cheesy bite!

## INGREDIENTS

¼ cup chopped onion

1 clove garlic, minced

¼ cup chopped bell pepper

2 tablespoons chicken broth

1 sweet chili pepper, minced

1½ cups diced cooked chicken

½ cup shredded cheddar cheese

½ cup shredded Monterey Jack cheese

non-stick cooking spray

4 flour tortillas

## TOOLS

sharp knife

cutting board

measuring cups

measuring spoons

frying pan

mixing spoon

mixing bowls

pot holders

spatula

1. Put the onion, garlic, bell pepper, and chicken broth in the frying pan. Cook over medium heat for 8 minutes. Add the chili pepper. Cook for 3 minutes. Stir in the chicken. Put the mixture in a bowl.

2. Put the cheeses in a separate bowl. Stir them together.

3. Wash the frying pan. Grease it with cooking spray. Set the pan over medium heat. Put a tortilla in the pan. Sprinkle half of the cheese mixture on the tortilla. Add half of the chicken mixture.

4. Cover the chicken mixture with another tortilla. Cook for 3 minutes. Flip it over. Cook for another 3 minutes.

5. Repeat steps 3 and 4 to make another quesadilla.

1

3

4

# GRILLED
# Chicken Kabobs

Veggies and meat on a stick? Yes, please!

## INGREDIENTS

1 orange bell pepper
1 red bell pepper
1 onion
4 chicken breasts, cubed
2 cups cubed pineapple
1 cup teriyaki sauce
2 tablespoons honey

## TOOLS

sharp knife
cutting board
measuring cups & spoons
wooden skewers
plate
small bowl
whisk
grill
basting brush

1. Soak the skewers in water for 30 minutes. Cut the peppers and onion into 2-inch (5 cm) squares.

2. Push a piece of chicken on a skewer. Add a red bell pepper square. Add an orange bell pepper square. Add an onion square. Add a cube of pineapple. Keep adding ingredients to the skewers. Fill as many skewers as you can. Set them on a plate.

3. Put the teriyaki sauce and honey in the bowl. Whisk them together.

4. Put the kabobs on the grill over high heat. Brush them with sauce. Turn the kabobs and brush them with more sauce. Keep turning and brushing them for 15 minutes, or until the chicken is done.

# Conclusion

Explore the world of chicken dishes. What else can you cook up?

Main dishes are fun to make and share! Feel proud of the dishes you prepare. Eat them with your family and friends. Chicken is one of many great ingredients for main dishes. Don't stop with chicken. Try other ingredients too!

# Glossary

**dessert** – a sweet food, such as fruit, ice cream, or pastry, served after a meal.

**entice** – to make someone want to do or have something.

**permission** – when a person in charge says it's okay to do something.

**savory** – having a strong, pleasing flavor that is not sweet.

**thaw** – to melt or unfreeze.

**utensil** – a tool used to prepare or eat food.

# WEBSITES

To learn more about Cool Main Dishes, visit **booklinks.abdopublishing.com**. These links are routinely monitored and updated to provide the most current information available.

# Index